Hunting and Fishing

Bird Hunting

Diane Bailey

Lerner Publications ◆ Minneapolis

Lerner Publications Company
An imprint of Lerner Publishing Group, Inc.
241 First Avenue North
Minneapolis, MN 55401 USA

For reading levels and more information, look up this title at www.lernerbooks.com.

Main body text set in Adrianna Regular.
Typeface provided by Chank.

Library of Congress Cataloging-in-Publication Data

Names: Bailey, Diane, 1966–author.
Title: Bird hunting / Diane Bailey.
Description: Minneapolis : Lerner Publications, [2024] | Series: Searchlight books - hunting and fishing | Includes bibliographical references and index. | Audience: Ages 8–11 | Audience: Grades 4–6 | Summary: "Turkeys, pheasants, ducks, and geese are all kinds of birds that are hunted. Bird hunting has a long history. Discover the gear that is used, how to stay safe while hunting, and more"—Provided by publisher.
Identifiers: LCCN 2022043932 (print) | LCCN 2022043933 (ebook) | ISBN 9781728491530 (library binding) | ISBN 9798765603727 (paperback) | ISBN 9798765600313 (ebook)
Subjects: LCSH: Fowling—Juvenile literature.
Classification: LCC SK315 .B35 2024 (print) | LCC SK315 (ebook) | DDC 799.2/4—dc23/eng/20230111

LC record available at https://lccn.loc.gov/2022043932
LC ebook record available at https://lccn.loc.gov/2022043933

Manufactured in the United States of America
3-1010664-51102-2/13/2024

Table of Contents

Chapter 1

GOING BIRD HUNTING

A gaggle of geese dabble in the water, looking for fish. The hunter waits for geese to take flight. Suddenly, a gust of wind startles the geese. They honk in alarm, lift their wings, and soar into the air. As they come into the range, the hunter is ready.

CANADA GEESE ARE LARGE BIRDS KNOWN FOR
MAKING A DISTINCTIVE HONKING NOISE.

Land and Water

There are two main types of game birds. Upland birds include turkeys, pheasants, grouse, doves, quail, woodcock, and partridges. They live on land that is higher, or up, from the waterline of nearby ponds and lakes. Upland birds usually like dense grass or brush that gives them safe places to nest and hide from predators.

Waterfowl include ducks, geese, coots, and other birds. Waterfowl spend some of their time in ponds, lakes, or marshes. Many eat grains like corn and wheat, so they are also found in fields where crops grow.

Hunting History

In the 1800s, it was a popular tradition to go hunting on Christmas. In 1900, bird expert Frank Chapman suggested people take that day off from hunting. Instead, he wanted them to count birds on Christmas. That would help people keep track of bird populations. In the first year, 27 people took part. The idea caught on, and now thousands of people do it.

The Christmas Bird Count started to emphasize the importance of conservation.

Gear Up

To find birds, hunters often use bird calls, small instruments that mimic the natural sounds birds make. For waterfowl, hunters also set up decoys on the water. Decoys are basically fake birds that attract real birds. They can be a simple, flat cutout or a fancy 3-D model.

It's possible to hunt birds with a bow and arrow, but most hunters choose a shotgun. A shotgun releases a burst of small pellets, called shot. They scatter as they are released from the gun. That gives the hunter a better chance to hit the target.

Taking Aim

Birds get spooked easily, so hunters do not want to get too close to them. A scope on their gun brings small, faraway objects into focus. A rangefinder is another helpful device. It measures the distance between the hunter and the prey. This way hunters don't risk taking shots from too far away.

KEEPING IT SAFE

A bird hunter's best protection is to be easily visible. Most states require hunters to wear bright, blaze orange clothing on their upper body. This could be a jacket, vest, or cap. Other hunters can easily see them, but the orange color doesn't bother the birds. Birds are more likely to avoid things that are shiny and reflect light. They also notice sound and movement.

Bright orange clothing helps hunters spot other hunters.

Some waterfowl hunters stay on land, but others like to go out in boats. That puts them closer to the game, but it is also riskier. A sudden movement to get a shot can make you lose your balance or tip the boat. It's important to wear a personal flotation device that will keep you above water if you fall in.

Firearm Safety

A gun safety course gives hunters the knowledge they need to prevent accidents. It teaches them how to use a weapon safely and with confidence. Hunters usually put in hours of target practice to improve their aim and skill using a gun. They know not to raise their gun until they are ready to shoot. They never point it at someone else, even if it's not loaded.

During an actual hunt, hunters only take shots that are in their zone of fire. The zone of fire is the area in which a hunter can shoot safely. For example, three hunters can walk next to each other in a line. The one in the middle will only shoot straight ahead, and the two on the sides will each cover birds that fly on their side of the line. This keeps everyone safe and makes it more likely to hit a target.

Chapter 3

BIRD HUNTING BASICS

Upland bird hunters spend a lot of time walking. They often search for birds through thick grass and brush. Birds are good at hiding, so hunters sometimes need help to locate them.

Bird calls imitate sounds like a turkey's gobble or a pheasant's cackle. Hunters use these to get real birds to answer back. That helps them figure out where they are. For waterfowl, many hunters set out decoys on the water. When ducks and geese see the decoys, they come over to join them.

HUNTERS USE DECOYS
AND BIRD CALLS TO HUNT PREY.

Dogs are a Hunter's Best Friend

Wild birds scare easily. They can be hard to sneak up on. That's where dogs can be a big help. Many hunting dogs have excellent smell. They can sniff out birds in hiding. Then they flush, or chase, them into the open. Then the hunter can get a clear shot. Some dogs also retrieve the bird once the hunter has taken it down.

When it comes time to shoot, hunters must make a decision. They can shoot birds when they are on the ground or in the water, or they can wait until they are flying. The skill of hitting flying targets with a shotgun is called wingshooting. Many hunters think this is more sportsmanlike. It is also more challenging!

Hunting History

Up until the early 1900s, many bird hunters kept live ducks and geese to use as decoys. Their calls would attract wild birds, making it easier to hunt. Live decoys were outlawed in the United States in 1935. By that time, there was so much hunting that wild birds couldn't keep up. Their numbers were decreasing. Officials decided that hunters had to use fake decoys to keep it fair to the birds.

Live decoys are no longer used in hunting.

Habits and Habitats

There are dozens of game birds that can be hunted at different times of year. Bird hunters get familiar with the habitats that different birds live in. Chukar partridge like rolling hills and fields of short grass. Pheasants can often be found among taller grasses on the edges of crop fields. Turkeys use open fields for feeding and mating. But they are much larger than other birds, so they sometimes take cover among trees.

Colder weather causes many birds to migrate to warmer areas. They travel on routes, or flyways, that are good places for hunters to find game.

Weather is another important factor. When it gets cold, birds often get more active as they search for food. Wind can also help hunters. It helps disguise a hunter's sound and smell. A lot of bird hunters think that the worse the weather, the better the hunting.

STEM Spotlight

Hunters traditionally used shot made from lead. Lead is dense and heavy. That helps it travel farther from a gun than shot made from other metals. But lead is bad for the environment and poisonous to animals and people. Steel shot is safer, but it weighs less and doesn't travel as far. To solve the problem, engineers designed pouches that can hold steel shot together longer. Less shot gets scattered around, and more reaches the target.

Lead contaminates water sources and is illegal to use for hunting waterfowl.

HUNTING AND CONSERVATION

In the 1800s and 1900s, many bird species died out because too many people hunted them. Today, birds face new threats. All over the world, climate is changing. That is making some birds' natural habitats too hot or too cold, or too wet or too dry. Sometimes other animals move in. They can prey on the birds or use up their food sources. People are always building new houses, shopping centers, and roads that chip away at natural habitats.

Birds are an important part of the environment. Keeping them safe helps keep other species safe. Hunters are part of this important job.

A Healthy Environment

Game birds can only be hunted during a certain season. That is when there are usually the most of them and they are not breeding. Hunters also must stay within a certain bag limit that says how many birds they can take at one time.

Hunters buy a license from their state that gives them permission to hunt. State officials then use this money to help preserve habitats where birds live. For example, they might clean up the water or plant trees. They also conduct studies to determine how many animals, and which kinds, live in a certain area. If there are too many, they might encourage hunting of a certain species to reduce their numbers. If there are too few, they might restrict hunting on that animal until the population numbers bounce back.

Keeping the land and animals healthy is part of
practicing conservation. If everyone works together,
hunters can enjoy the land now and in the future.

Hunting Hints

- Young hunters should always hunt with a responsible adult.

- Plan a pre-hunting trip to learn the landscape and observe animal habits.

- Don't ignore short grass or thin cover. Birds can hide in very small places.

- When using decoys, arrange them with a space in the middle for birds to land in.

- When firing into a flock of birds, pick one to focus on. That will give you a better shot.

Birds are good at hiding in nature.

Glossary

conservation: protecting resources like land and water, and using them wisely

decoy: an imitation bird used to attract other birds

flush: forcing game from cover

gaggle: a flock of geese

game: animals hunted for food or sport

habitat: the environment a particular animal lives in

population: the total number of a type of animal

predator: an animal that hunts and eats other animals

upland: an area of higher land

waterfowl: birds that live on or around water

wingshooting: shooting birds while they are flying

zone of fire: the area that each hunter in a group may shoot in

Learn More

Bailey, Diane. *Small Game Hunting*. Minneapolis: Lerner Publications, 2024.

Carpenter, Tom. *Upland Bird Hunting*. Lake Elmo, MN: Focus Readers, 2018.

Doyle, Abby Badach. *Turkey Hunting*. New York: Gareth Stevens Publishing, 2023.

How Sport Hunting Works
https://adventure.howstuffworks.com/outdoor-activities/hunting/alternative-methods/sport-hunting.htm

Kiddle: Upland Hunting Facts for Kids
https://kids.kiddle.co/Upland_hunting

Know It All: The Hunt
https://knowitall.org/video/hunt-natural-state

Index

Photo Acknowledgments

Image Credits: p. 5; Wirestock Creators/Shutterstock, p. 6; Alamin-Khan/Shutterstock, p. 7; Sam Lee/Dreamstime, p. 8; Bob Hilscher/iStock Photos, p. 9; Jarihin/Dreamstime, p. 10; Komilovdream/Dreamstime, p., 11; gan chaonan/Shutterstock, p. 13; Maksim Safaniuk/Shutterstock, p. 14; Poppypixstock/Dreamstime, p. 15; Steve Oehlenschlager/Shutterstock, p. 17; dasytnik/Shutterstock, p. 18-19; otsphoto, p. 20; RelentlessImages/Shutterstock, p. 21; Shawn Milne/Dreamstime, p. 22; Tanvir Parves Ahmed/iStock Photos, p. 23; Click98/Shutterstock, p. 25; M600i/Shutterstock, p. 26; Brian Lasenby/Dreamstime, p. 27; StexP/Shutterstock, p. 28; Aila Bond/Shutterstock, p. 29; Ksenia Raykova/Dreamstime.

Cover: Stephen Oehlenschlager/Dreamstime.